ILMARINEN VOGEL

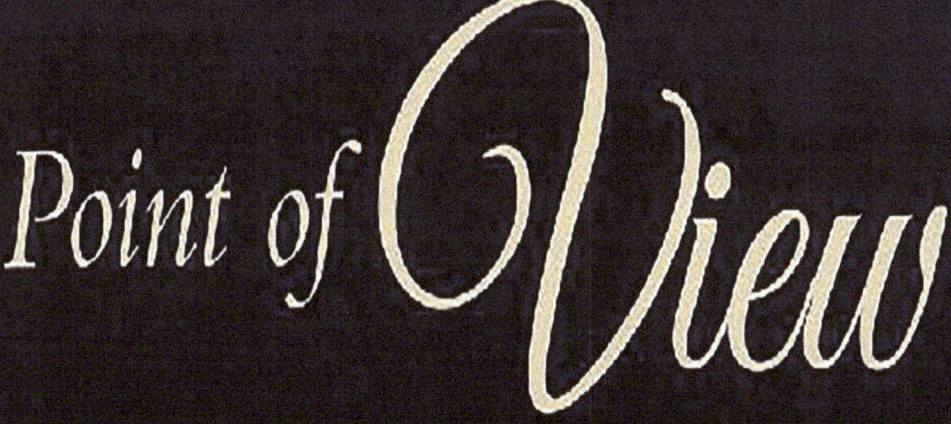

Point of View

A WALK THROUGH NATURE AND MY THOUGHTS

Studio of Books LLC
5900 Balcones Drive Suite 100
Austin, Texas 78731
www.studioofbooks.org
Hotline: (254) 800-1183

Ordering Information:
Special discounts are available on quantity purchases by corporations, associations, and others. For details, contact the publisher at the address above.

Printed in the United States of America.

| ISBN-13: | Softcover | 978-1-964864-77-8 |
| | eBook | 978-1-964864-78-5 |

Library of Congress Control Number: : 2024923450

ILMARINEN VOGEL

POINT OF VIEW

A WALK THROUGH NATURE AND MY THOUGHTS

Contents

Point of View

The Flow

who is crossing the bridge

should I go with the flow

am I safe with the fence

should I wait for the snow

can I trust my desire

do I have enough passion

will my tent last the season

is my gear still in fashion

all of this is good reason

to escape acts of treason

to outlast all the lies

and to tie some new ties

4

I invite you to wander along with me

the ultimate riches lie in sharing the bounty

as nature is demonstrating by giving

without asking questions

Promise

it can lift us

it can crush us

inspiration starts

with showing up

tread lightly

look cautiously

be part of the light

cast your own shadow

share what you see

never be alone

that promise is kept

every day of our life

Rose

A rose who in her simple beauty
will stand the test of time forever
sometimes we even get the scent
bees know the rose can feed a queen
the bee is key to life and clever
bees know what the creator meant
some of us know that with a rose
we can say things no words can tell
and please the nose to show the one
we love with rose's everlasting spell
that we will hold them high above
we ask the rose the rose will tell

Life

the glacier scrubbed the rock face clean
the earth was crushed beneath a mile
of ice that slowly melted back
oh look new life has got a smile
and nature wants to turn it green

Mist

each day at sunrise and at dusk

the ocean sends a gift to life

it rises with a gentle breeze

and moisture settles

life has ways and lust for life

to sprout and to create with ease

Standing Tall

I stand on top of cadillac
I see the sea
from mountain's back
the polished rock
is dressed in green
and very fragrant
granite islands
one and all change color
Summer Spring and Fall
the winter is a wonderland
I stand in awe I gaze afar
my life at home has ended
out here I'm home I'm not offended
and life can deal another hand
I stand alone on my own terms
no longer stranger in another's land

Pink Granite

when vikings landed here in quest
of treasure maidens and the rest
of all the things that made them ship
across the oceans take the trip
as all they found was granite pink
it made them homesick sad and tired
no treasure here few girls were sired
soon they went home to feast and drink

View

I have a cannon have a view
seems there is nothing I can't do
I have no knees have no good hips
I do have eyes can still take trips

to play a part build a new world
miss nothing what I find out here
is mine to play that's all I care
I use my eyes go anywhere

I fall in love with things I see
all by myself for once I'm free
no one to dare get mad at me
that's how it is as it should be

far out to sea my eyes are gazing
heart feeling free it is amazing
joy and contentment nature's art
horizon gone, I'm feeling smart

can sense a world that lies beyond
feel free to make up my own story
with my fair share of homemade glory
and all the drama I might want

Horizon

is it a vision

or my destination

is it distracting me

from what is right before my toes

what must I suffer or endure

go far beyond to find a cure

to reach my own horizon

will there be yet another one

once I have seen and reached the summit

I will believe my eyes for sure

Dream

about a sailboat was my dream
with shallow draft and wide of beam
a sturdy hull to weather gales
a pleasant rig with painted sails
was in the tidal flow at anchor
where I could rock my love in arm
was holding pace with natures ways
here I would last for days and days

This Life Is Art

come look today the fleet is out

see whales and dolphins come to play

the fishing fleet can lay in port

to rest their weary bones

they call it Sunday anyway

and everyone can do their part

this life is good

this life is art

Take a Peek

I see horizons near and far
some are so faint they make me wonder
what our world might look like yonder
where trees are clinging to a rock
there might be people shack and dock
and all the beauty they behold
far greater than what I was told
I might get spellbound dare I look?
to me the world says take a peek
it might be more than what you seek
and beauty in the eye of the beholder
is likely that which makes you bolder

Safe World

come look a giant built a wall

and we will never take a fall

as long as we believe the tale

that our world will never fail

as long as we agree to fear

the next guy who will soon appear

and claim the trail beneath our feet

we will be strangers 'till we meet

Olympus

I see the world olympus style
as humans fear you all the while
up in your cloud life with a view
checking out others what they do
some of them dare explore the odds
that they might risk the wrath of gods
while I have all the fun or not
well just relax smoke some more pot

Lucky Ones

we are the lucky ones who have the senses

to smell and see and feel the thrill

of nature's gifts laid out to all

from early spring to late in fall

then water turns to brilliant stars

some call it heaven others snow

some took up close and see the crystals

unique each one to hold a story

of former life and future glory

this is the secret of the show

This Is Not Mars

these icy storms freeze skin on nose
freeze hand freeze face freeze all my toes
are sure to end all life up here
give life a chance and do not fear
look how the rocks are giving room
cracks from the frost are open wide
so seeds and roots can sneak inside
find moisture left from frozen doom
set up a cozy growing womb
and sprouts seek light and ache for room
where snow melt trickles sometimes flows
holds memory as it gives moisture
where all the living cells are hearts
are organisms made from stars
immersed within the epic fight
of shadow crevice dust and light
where nourishment gives form to life
defining earth in love not strife
this is the romance of the stars
on planet earth this is not mars

Living Things

the world presents us much to think
consider what we eat or drink
we are inventing words for all we watch some walk
we see some crawl
yet instantly we sort the show by things we see
and things we know
soon we tell things from living beings
feel very proud choose who has feelings
I stand there asking did I look
did I take note of what it took
when did I lose my sense of joy
lose all the power be a toy
can I foresee these many things
and comprehend the interaction
or have a sense of what it brings
when I consider my dissection
I start by seeing the design
I stand in awe I let it shine
see time and space see life in action
me just a part a minor fraction
oh yes I can and yes I might
lay on my back look up at night
to see the dance of many players
I now will join on many layers
to earn the rank of living things
or lift me with eternal wings

Tiny

I stand atop a massive granite block
that used to be the biggest mountain
which had to yield to power of the ice
that piled mile high and took it down
in chunks soon to be ground to dust
to sand and rubble forming islands
reaching waters north to south
fighting winds and tides and glacier flows
long time to reach their destination
before the ice began to melt
ten thousand freezing Years ago
now tiny pools of water tiny rivulets
feed tiny plants grow tiny seeds
right in the face of epic storms
from major frost events to
blistering heat and thunderstorms
awaiting temperate seasons
as champions of life they are
hungry for another day another reason
for love of life devoted to a noble art
with generosity of sharing and of giving
that which makes our tiny seedling
bigger than our daily life which conquers
ending life and causes tiny signs of living

Success

I entertain a thought or two
and watch what nature likes to do
to balance failure and success
can see the greening see the mess
I overlook that in the dying
lie secrets that present to life
new opportunities I would be lying
did I not show you this success

I See

with tele-lens I seek to see
let memory connect the dots
where boots touched rock
where hands grabbed hold
remembering the sound of life
where music real and eternal
is present giving me permission
to live forgive feel love again
remembering the life I knew
and part of me that never could
forget how much I once have been
out here at home inside my world
thrilled with this place I saw for one
who was at risk of losing my own spirit
come home to share the best of everything I see
connect the green on rocks including you and me
take stock of life that's left in me
my memory has put me here
where I lost nothing where I found
that sharing all that I can see
will make me whole
will take me home
will bring you out
will bring me in

How Life Should Be

earth is an organism just like mine
slow down enough so I can see
earth giving hope to those she crushed
by mile high ice that sank the crust
into its lava bath and there it floats
now rising half an inch a Year
new life emerges as the rock is fractured
and the globe repairs the dent
to watch the fight of life on mount desert
despite its harsh environment inspires me
this spirit is a sign of nature
not fight for senseless domination
look closely see the dance of organisms
a tango making room for one another
creating living space impossible to see
just who came first who made it possible
for next of kin to fill the new formed cracks
with brand new life so once again
I learn how life begins to be

A Dream

I had a dream one stormy night
it was pitch black yet it was bright
it flashed before my sleeping mind
as bright as if in real sight
an Arab stallion reared and rose
before an eagle on the ground
they both looked startled as the
flash revealed the mighty shapes
the thunder clap that followed soon
like crushing splintering a tree
a victim of the flash and thunder
of uncontrolled electric energy

the horse came down the bird rose up
a dance of light and thunder clap
of wings and hooves of neck and beak
seen in the flashes of the light
they were the power of the night
no limit to the force of strikes
of hooves or wings an epic fight
the fast retort as fast as lightning

as fast and hard as sonic booms
two creatures of the day and night
in thunder clap in lightning flash

were dancing here from flash to crash
from thunderclap to blinding light
as spellbound I observed the show
of my two favorite creatures dancing
a dance too frightening to behold
so dangerously close and bold
I thought it was a dream

One More Fruit

The life I did encounter on this rock

was stunningly complex and beautiful

was scented and was full of elegance

it seemed like life was now attempting

to close another cycle in the season

another fruit another blossom

in deed the ants the bees the butterflies

the bushes and the trees the grasses

the heather stood together saying

let one more cycle be complete

for one more fruit

Swaying In The Arms Of Life

just as I think there is no life

no use to fight and struggle any more

no language to persuade my next of kin

that what I did was not a sin

was not the act I had in mind

was not the life I had designed

the struggle did not even cover

my failure as a mate or lover

I was no longer reaching her

had lost the contact to her heart

the kisses went unanswered in the end

the flow had stopped no telling where it went

but look there is much life out there

it's full of color everywhere

inviting curiosity and contact

with scent and touch with sound and taste

there is much life no sense to waste

another day in grieving sorrow

all that I see it has tomorrow
has beauty style and invitation
to play to buzz make love and feel
the inner strength the sex appeal
is oozing out to touch and feel
the willing dancers at the ball
as long as music plays there is no strife
I keep swaying in the arms of Life

To You

give me water give me pebbles
give me time am not a fool
I will grind with waters current
endless patience makes a pool
I will fill it with my love
which I dedicate to you

Eden

like new found love

the tiny things that make it last

must be assembled and collected

some need to grow, some wander in

some fly right in to find the fertile ground

some even stay to nurture soil for life

some hold the moisture soften rocks

some eat the insects some attract them

a talent pool that grows with time

the more retained the more it holds

the pleasure is all mine these days

you're not too old the wise man says

and slow and steady there she goes

the home of Eden slowly shows

like new found love from head to toes

Moon

look at the world from the moon with me
see blue white red and so much green
tell me all that you feel in your heart as you see
she basks in the sun with life in her glee
has water galore wonder what she will do
has things that are moving some lay still as a stone
she sends floods of water grinding bowls into rock
making powder and sand feeding algae and moss
growing roots leaving baths for the birds
they drop seeds sprouting plants to sustain
every movable feast from flyer to beast
that can hide in the green dreaming large
with desire to take a sip from the bowl
climbing up a bit higher to look at the moon
see the two of us gazing at earth and her brood
lust for water and life feeling hunger for food
join us there come on down to the permanent feast
you come down here to stay for a fortnight at least

Now

deep in my mind is a place to which I can turn

the race stops there and silence rules

when something I must learn

I go there when the world is spinning fast

I see no point in winning races to undefined

horizons when no one can define a reason

for nothing in the end it feels like such trend

to race and race and race and race

is keeping me in running motion no time to stop

and see the beauty find the treasure on the way

that nothing lives in plain sight here for all to see

so everyone can touch and feel

can sense the color smell the scent can

contemplate just what it meant to know the moment

of creation to witness making of the world

to hear the wind the rain sensation

that left in awe me as I went

I gaze into this image how

I wrinkle nose I wrinkle brow I stick my chin out

into space and reaffirm my steady gaze

for here am I and this is now

Wealth

I look at green and red and black
it pulls me in it sets me back
it leaves an image of a rose
when afterwards my eyes I close
in wonderment I feel the strength
of green to give a boost to aid
my fragile state to lift my fate
from nothing up to go the length
I am in touch with every fiber
of my existence and I feel
the corresponding health appeal
of green and red and gold and black
this is the wealth that brings me back

Let It Be

a lightning strike took out this tree

so much alike that which struck me

it made it look like it's the ending for one

more creature there's no mending

what nature took in one big bang

surprising where my birds once sang

of nesting laying eggs and resting from

feeding offspring now its testing

new ways of taking a new stand

close to the ground creative hand

in concert with a million sources

no sound to hear nothing to see

for savages like you and me

who think to strike the final inning

in nature it's a new beginning

it takes a God to let it be

I could stay

the challenge is to stand alone
and face the world as from a throne
of heightened clarity and vision
to come to many a decision
from what to do and where to go
to what to hide and what to show
to make a new determination
to integrate or flee damnation
how can I get around the trap
and close the ever present gap
of compromise from self to fate
can I now risk and make a date?
if I don't stand the test of time
and have to spin upon a dime
the door was shown me from inside
that made me run go far and wide
the outside is my safest place
no challenge to my mind out here
I see my grace and life of strength
in nature's way if that is true
then I can stay

rest

grass looks so green across the fence
remember when you feel all tense
then lay down on your back and gaze
into the clouds and through the haze
the green across the fence looks best
from where you are now you can rest

Vernal Pools

in life we too have vernal pools
they work the same as nature's do
they do collect the stuff of life
from everywhere and hope to thrive
they too are not the well fed kind
the threat of drying up the mind
if no one stays to feed the flow
for our vernal pool to grow
stay calm a mirror to behold
the sky above and a reflection
of those you love and those who left
go look see for yourself I'm told

Not The Moon

the love that you and I are feeling

is hidden from our eyes in ways

that we don't see the light for days

and can't observe just how it plays

we think a lot have many feelings

but if we don't express them soon

we may forget in all our dealings

that this is earth and not the moon

To Be

the fractured granite face it flows
just slow enough so no one knows
that is how come we have no feel
for such a massive moving deal
we dig it up we cut and polish stone
we shape it carve it hone it smooth
we treat it just like modeling clay
we haul it put it on display
I like to see it rest in peace
let other life forms have their way
and work the fractured blocks to please
my plants my seeds let flowers have a say
this drama of the gifted world is glee
right here right now just right for me
I am in awe with deep respect I see
the urgency that makes me want to be

For Life

trees holding on to rocks
are showing us how life prevails
through storms through ice and when it hails
we measure the audacity of life we come to see
what secrets we can glean from this display
for us who seem to struggle endlessly to stay
together through the winds of time
the rain and ice storms we create
in our ignorance of nature as we hate
that which is foreign is the yarn we torture
instead of watching this display of nature
where different creatures work to nurture
the harmony that can withstand the storm
by clinging helpful to a secret norm
of handing life support and not a claim
to dominate to rule to shame
the weakest ones who cannot name
the power they can gather here
where nature lives for life
and not for fear

Possibilities

nature shows us how life is nurtured
by mutual support not competition
a symphony of diverse organisms
creating and recreating one another
moving forward by reacting
and working hand in hand providing
opportunity in celebrating life
of endless new found possibilities

Desire To Give

Fertility is the result of an unquenchable thirst
and desire to give more than to take from life's table
each gift opens a world for all participants
to share with nature and humans alike
this could be taught in school
the benefit of people and nature
sharing a livable planet
with a sustainable future and an economy
that works for all
technology used to free people
to create more time for art
gardening writing reading and travel
we need to find our way to a social order
that does not serve only the interests of shareholders
but considers the interests of stakeholders
one that can focus on the needs of people and nature
it is the only way to make the numbers work

Love is life

love is the human experience
that proves that the more we practice it
the more there is to go around
it works that way in nature
each organism leaves something
for the next to convert and to raise it
to the next level of fertility and growth
it creates a relay that spreads
like a good idea
that love is life and life in love.

Open Wide

as earth rebounds
from melting a mile of ice
granite opens wide
to receive a little dust
that gives home to seeds
to sprout and grow into new trees

Rocky Beginnings

tiny rock pools are grinding bowls

use running water to motivate

deepening pools

collecting moisture

nourishing life

humans think they own water

genes and other human lives

forgetting we all came from here

and if we don't remember

we will return

and start the cycle of life again

for newborn creatures to emerge

where once we had our chance

and we might reemerge

in another billion years

Giving

I stand before the building blocks of life
what does it take? more war? more strife?
or can I find a way that works for all
no need to take another deadly fall
I see a glimpse of hope where I observe
how Nature goes about the task of living
it does not look as much like taking
in deed it looks a lot like giving

Blueberry And Rose

A bell shaped blossom
and a tiny rose
are gathering from their creation
the energy for those
who take it from the petals
to the feast
where in the dance of life
a fruit will grow
that feeds a hungry beast
and that is almost all we know

Birch

the birch a pioneering plant
can spread its seeds upon by the wind
can stand the coldest climate
brave brutal storms and dares
to hold its own before the rest
of nature comes to join
some build a nest some use its shade
some join the humus building trade
it is a mother tree of sorts
with all the favors that it sports
its sap makes tonic some make beer
and everyone has cause to cheer

Invitation

when nothing else you have to give
a single rose will do
just ask the bees they know to live
intoxicated by the scent
that speaks to our heart and more
it is the key to any door

What If

what if there were no fence for me
if I could pick out where to be
could travel far and wide to see
the other side of every coin
and turn another page of every book
to learn about the human race
the hidden places I could find
a different life a state of mind

Another Feast

when snow had melted

winter gone

and soil was softened by the frost

some seeds arrived aboard a bird

and droppings fell

the bird was glad that it had lost

its cargo stemming from a feast

that gave it power to come here

and leave a gift that did not cost

a dime a nickel or a cent

it simply dropped and there it went

fell into soil and grew another host

for yet another feast

Just Be

I look at water mind absorbed in musings
I see the world and ask where I might fit
how I was meant to be and how to act
who gave me my confusing orders
go here or there do this and that
learn all the skills to fit the task
I don't know who but still I ask
who is the ghost behind this mask
who is the happiest of all hosts
and who enjoys his task the most
am I beholden to some master
who let me stand and watch the act
to work and struggle when in fact
I asked if I could help to make things happen
I walked away with new acquired skills
one day who knows they might come handy
here at the shore above the tidal plain
great things are happening and here
my mentorship begins anew with Nature's fun
the bliss and joy of life is tangible
they did have strife here as I've seen

from water's edge high up the rocks

creation still in progress

and yes I'm here there is a reason

come see what else there is to learn

once I can be the eyes the heart the pulse the glee

this is no longer limited to me

I'm just a part of this sensation.

I say just be.

Recovery

Crushed stones were pounded and
diminished drowned waterlogged
split and demolished like this tree
just like the tree the rock the sea and battered me
what better model could there be
we all have met in life before
but now I ask you is there more?
can water sand and wood conspire
to start new life another fire?
I open both my eyes and look
my nose takes in the scent and sounds
there's life before me it is meant to render me
in nature's arms with many species' endless charms
to coddle me and make me lose the fear
because what nature's toolbox has in store for me
to play with it is here to take and love it is all here
and like the shore recovers so will I

Love And Death

seaweed softens rocks

gives food and shelter to countless creatures

keeps promises to life and samples

currents of the tides for more

this century low tide will cause a hundred year high

for sharing and tearing reminding us that life

is space between love and death

forever coming forever leaving

t

No Man's Beach

family gathering and love

peace on Earth achieved

moments to remember

chuckles at stories

the discovery

that this might be a first and last gathering

moving memory of a happy moment

into memory of a family

for another hundred years

Still Life

still alive

a constellation

movement and action

interaction in time and space

plants minerals and crustations

seemingly unrelated connected by life

where do I fit into this picture is my question

I stand here feeling part of this collage right now

I smell the scent I see the image I feel the pleasure

of this picture now it is no longer still

I made it come alive

Deja Vue

tide waves flotsam sand
pebbles rocks bedrock crust
my eyes inseparably
connected to life
sometimes I walk away
choose different toys
yet every time I return
I have deja vue
part of me never left
and what I took
had all remained the same
yet it is different now
for I no longer am
who I was then
reunion is
an introduction
to now

Who He Is

the eyes of nature
her designs and genius
left for dead by the blind
found alive by the lucky one
who stumbled upon this treasure
of universe shaped and reproduced
right here for the returning seeker to find
he is not lonely on this planet but always home
for color and texture show him part of who he is

Chair And Wine

come in she said

I made a house for us

I architected it

with not much fuss

this lacy cozy love affair

has been through many storms

and to be fair

it has endured the test of time

most of the wood is either gone

or is still there

so come on in

bring chair and wine

Tell Me More

did you come up from iron core

how did you get away

why are you not sinking

but you keep on coming up

how did you beat gravity

do you have a will

tell me more

Living Things

I sense long stories in this book
the layers tell of the desire
to sort all substance by a plan
that someday can reveal itself
when life becomes organic
enrich my sorted mineral store
come power energy and more
all stay together under pressure
now getting ready to partake
and build

Story

when there was heat

a planet molten to the core

and substance was distilled from cosmic power

merge interact dream from a distant past

to forge a future from the fire

when cooling seemed the only way to hold

a steady path and stay

in living distance to the star

that gave this planet life and ample water

to cool and nourish living cells that could maintain

the heat and the desire to dream of magic from

above until they found a way to sort

and separate the living world to be supported

to sustain to fill the space with lasting life

from love above to death beneath

to function in a living cycle

from love to birth to growth to seed

to stay in flux enough

to heed the memory of life

and dream creatively

to take a lot but give a little more

Another Look

land usually submerged
like feelings we keep covered
until surprise events can lay them bare
like rocks and gravel in a lunar tide
this is my chance to take another look

Driftwood

Like lines in faces of the old

express life

and much of history

stories are told in the lines of logs

new life is moving into crevices

while hard spines of the structure still resist

making visible the architecture of life

supporting parts of plant life

clues in colors of logs

new purpose is emerging

flotsam gets washed up on sand bars

high above the regular highwater mark

creating barriers for quiet places

with humus and fresh water

where countless organisms thrive

Tangible

components of myself

ready and willing to engage

performance

of miracles

interaction

of substance and energy

· joined by the audacity of life

make it tangible

Snapshot

seeing work that took ten thousand years to do

it took a mile-high pile of ice

with pressure great enough to kneed this chunk of

clay like dough

took long enough to turn it into rock

the weight of ice pressed on the globe rebounding

I witness work in progress now

creatures have resided here as climate changed

us humans are the recent ones

am one of them try get my arms around it

am by myself with family and friends in the wings

will I find the words to show my gratitude

or will I turn to rock before I do?

slow forces

creation is a work in progress
and not part of history we learn
now it is part of life as it emerges
integrated in this process I discern
I own the gift of sensing signs of life
I see smell taste I hear and even feel
I own the gift of curiosity and learning
acquiring skills to share my observations
inherited ability and urge to be creative
I train the heart to visualize the yet unseen
born with the genius to ask some valid questions
that let me journey far and sound the deep
I cultivate and study ways to serve
pass on responsibility to conserve
am privileged to honor God's creation
to hold this precious gift in trust

Intelligent Universe

The softer side emerges

where sand is trapping water

and roots are taking hold dissolving minerals

with help from countless tiny creatures

sunlight creating ample nourishment

synthesizing and launching organisms

this still life of the ones that I can see

their beauty and their secrets give me pause

I share it even though I dare not touch it

the gift of life received in gratitude

to my intelligent universe

the heart of creation

beating strong

in me

now

Memory

the finest sand

the grit the pebbles

the rock that does not want to sink

the sticks the drift wood and the leafy greens

remind me of the many things that water does with life

we touch it and it will remember our very essence retain it always

like fingerprints in frozen state in liquid and in vapor longing

to surround the living cells of every living organism

giving every cell a sentient beating feeling heart

while foolishly I crown myself the king of this

invoking God and Son and holy Spirit

to make the case denying truth

that I became the only one

to claim the seat

of the creator

of life

book of life

it can lift us it can crush us

inspiration starts with showing up

tread lightly look cautiously

be part of the light cast your own shadow

share what you see never be alone

that promise will be kept every day of your life

beyond

there is a place for life reserved in every cell

ordained to be in conflict over space and time

as urgency to thrive appears to be a fight

and every cell is born a thinking creature

that has the genius to help to add

a species rather than suppress

what was already born

new life expectancy

lies hidden there

beyond

water

the miracle substance
densest just above freezing
expands when frozen
explodes when super-heated
as ice it floats
something continues beneath
there is more
there is
life

Between

love and death

are the outside points of our experience

many never felt love or made love

most have never even died

wonderment and fear

that is the space

where humans

try living

here

now

Flowchart

the chartroom at the library of life

displays some secrets that we need to know

to safely navigate the planet we call home

the flowchart is as valid a reminder

as we can find to realize

that slow looks still

to those who live

for less than

hundred

years

Emerging Life

where mountains meet the sea
I stand in awe before the facts of life
where floods and epic ebbs have washed
the picture clean on shore
now I can read the pages
never seen before
about emerging life

survival of the fittest

used to explain who is here and who is not

principles of selection and evolution

were articulated by the scientists

giving each other doctor titles

and handing out entitlement

to owners of privilege title

and right to dominate

strip pump hunt and

procure in terminal

harvest invoking

natural selection

Look Beyond

it is not far to get from here to there

the stories we are told by those

who claim to know

what's waiting yonder at the other shore

they came from things they saw

come from stories they were told

which is the sum of that which they behold

because we all begin our lives with a blank slate

or so the rumor has it look around

the things we see and things we understand

are not the same that others see and feel

I need to use my eyes to see what I can see

and that is not the same as what it seems to be

from other points of view that give me reason

to go a little further and to take a look

beyond the other shore

there might be things

no one should now ignore

there might be truth in facts

that no one knew before

that turn my story

into a store

Care

call it kismet

call it karma

what's the difference you ask

kismet is the offering

karma is what we do

and how it makes us feel

the glacier brought the rock

from northern mountains here

the rock pool ground a hollow in the stone

rain fills it with water

this is the kismet part of life

the offering was made as part of this creation

tides wash the bottom of the rock

rains fill shallow bowls with water

fresh water in the briny estuary is a gift to life

birds bees and dragon flies

birds spread seeds bees pollinate and dragon flies

consume mosquitos

that is karma at its purest form

presented here for me and to take note

another sign of life which gives me courage

to notice kismet and to care for karma

Success

water is the bearer of memory

present and essential

to all living things

inside and outside

of every living cell

delivers and removes

what is helpful or harmful

giving and receiving

energy transformed to substance

substance back to energy

no void between sentient and vegetative

wherever water is present

life can be delivered

as key to success

Audacity Of Life

a little water

a little crack in rock

a little salt

a little heat

a little seed

and life is back

One More Look

before I leave
take one more look
to imprint on my open mind
the tale of what it really took
to craft a world that makes a living
that can create and keep on giving

Merman

if I don't find a different way
it may get dark and I must stay
it may get cold it may be wet
it may be under water yet
and I am not yet qualified
to be a merman for the night

Looking Back

I look back at the mountain top
where all this musing had its start
I feel like I discovered art
up there I felt immensely tall
could take a leap could risk a fall
down here I now feel very small
a grain of sand no risk at all
am at the bottom of the tide
still looking for the other side

Another Shore

I could go back the way I came
It's not my purpose or my aim
I cannot leave this place in shame
the only option suitable to me
is to persist and find a path
the way of water using memory
to reach another shore
the way it has been tried and done
by countless immigrants before

Past And Future

the past leaves roots

the future needs more seed

plants do have ways to stay alive

send roots when shoots are sprouting

grow flowers feeding bees and growing seeds

let birds and wind deliver them to fertile ground

to give new growth a chance to root is kismet

seeding and sprouting being karma

but water is the gift of life

some call it love and I do too

Reflection

each crystal is a child of water
unique and ready to reflect the light
now we can see and do some thinking
and some reflecting of our own

www.ingramcontent.com/pod-product-compliance
Lightning Source LLC
Chambersburg PA
CBHW051207120626
46547CB00013B/1243